STARLINGS

by Nick Payne

SAMUEL FRENCH

Copyright © 2020 by Nick Payne
All Rights Reserved

STARLINGS is fully protected under the copyright laws of the British Commonwealth, including Canada, the United States of America, and all other countries of the Copyright Union. All rights, including professional and amateur stage productions, recitation, lecturing, public reading, motion picture, radio broadcasting, television and the rights of translation into foreign languages are strictly reserved.

ISBN 978-0-573-11663-6

concordtheatricals.co.uk

concordtheatricals.com

FOR AMATEUR PRODUCTION ENQUIRIES

UNITED KINGDOM AND WORLD
EXCLUDING NORTH AMERICA
licensing@concordtheatricals.co.uk
020-7054-7200

Each title is subject to availability from Concord Theatricals, depending upon country of performance.

CAUTION: Professional and amateur producers are hereby warned that *STARLINGS* is subject to a licensing fee. Publication of this play does not imply availability for performance. Both amateurs and professionals considering a production are strongly advised to apply to the appropriate agent before starting rehearsals, advertising, or booking a theatre. A licensing fee must be paid whether the title is presented for charity or gain and whether or not admission is charged.

This work is published by Samuel French Ltd, an imprint of Concord Theatricals.

The professional rights in this play are controlled by Curtis Brown Group Ltd, Haymarket House, 28-29 Haymarket, London SW1Y 4SP.

No one shall make any changes in this title for the purpose of production. No part of this book may be reproduced, stored in a retrieval system, or transmitted in any form, by any means, now known or yet to be invented, including mechanical, electronic, photocopying, recording, videotaping, or otherwise, without the prior written permission of the publisher. No one shall upload this title, or part of this title, to any social media websites.

The right of Nick Payne to be identified as author of this work has been asserted in accordance with Section 77 of the Copyright, Designs and Patents Act 1988.

MUSIC USE NOTE

Licensees are solely responsible for obtaining formal written permission from copyright owners to use copyrighted music in the performance of this play and are strongly cautioned to do so. If no such permission is obtained by the licensee, then the licensee must use only original music that the licensee owns and controls. Licensees are solely responsible and liable for all music clearances and shall indemnify the copyright owners of the play(s) and their licensing agent, Concord Theatricals, against any costs, expenses, losses and liabilities arising from the use of music by licensees. Please contact the appropriate music licensing authority in your territory for the rights to any incidental music.

IMPORTANT BILLING AND CREDIT REQUIREMENTS

If you have obtained performance rights to this title, please refer to your licensing agreement for important billing and credit requirements.

USE OF COPYRIGHT MUSIC

A licence issued by Concord Theatricals to perform this play does not include permission to use the incidental music specified in this copy. Where the place of performance is already licensed by the PERFORMING RIGHT SOCIETY (PRS) a return of the music used must be made to them. If the place of performance is not so licensed then application should be made to the PRS, 2 Pancras Square, London, N1C 4AG. A separate and additional licence from PHONOGRAPHIC PERFORMANCE LTD, 1 Upper James Street, London W1F 9DE (www.ppluk.com) is needed whenever commercial recordings are used.

FIRST PERFORMANCE INFO

The first performance of *Starlings* took place as part of the Royal Court Young Writers Festival 2009.

AUTHOR'S NOTE

This play has never received a professional production (it was performed as a semi-staged reading way back when in 2008 as part of the Royal Court's Young Writers Festival, directed by Natalie Ibu). Good luck.

CHARACTER

ARTHUR, male, born 1948.
MELISSA, female, born 1970.
LEE, male, born 1968.
RICHARD, male, born 1970.
LILLY, female, born 2002.

Two actresses should play Melissa: one in 1979 and another for the remainder of the play.

Two actors should play Lee: one in 1979 and another for the remainder of the play.

The actress who plays Melissa in 1979 should also play Lilly in 2008.

An interval could fall after 1999.

DECEMBER, 1979.

Hospital canteen. Evening. A large window runs across the back of the canteen. Fireworks are sporadically seen and heard as the scene progresses.

ARTHUR, *thirty one, and* **LEE**, *eleven.*

ARTHUR *is unpacking a large order of takeaway sausage and chips onto one of the tables.*

ARTHUR Vodka?

LEE Must've been four or five bottles.

ARTHUR *shakes his head a little.*

Where've you been?

ARTHUR You what?

LEE Where have you been?

ARTHUR Out.

LEE Where?

No response.

Thought we were gonna spend New Year's in?

ARTHUR Where's y'sister?

LEE Dad where've you been?

No response.

LEE *cries.*

ARTHUR *stops unpacking the takeaway.*

ARTHUR What you doing?

No response.

Stop fucking crying. Lee. Come on. Stop fucking crying.

LEE I just. Didn't know what to do.

ARTHUR Did the right thing, don't worry about it.

LEE Should've seen her though. The bottles and the mess on the stairs.

ARTHUR Have a beer.

LEE D'you know what it sounded like?

ARTHUR Lee.

LEE Do you though, d'you know what it sounded like?

No response.

You know when you hold a bag of flour and you drop it on the floor?

ARTHUR *opens a can of lager and hands it to* **LEE**.

LEE *drinks. Grimaces a little after.*

Didn't wanna look.

ARTHUR Why don't you go and get y'sister? Tell her y'tea's ready?

LEE Somebody screamed. Fat bird in number eleven. Heard her.

Where've you been?

ARTHUR Out.

LEE But where?

ARTHUR Sit down and eat y'dinner.

LEE *and* **ARTHUR** *sit at the table and eat.*

LEE Got any vinegar?

ARTHUR *reaches into his jacket pocket and pulls out a chip shop bottle full of vinegar.*

Where'd you get that?

No response.

's it nicked? Did you nick it from the chip shop?

ARTHUR D'you want the fucking thing or don't ya?

LEE *puts vinegar on his chips.*

LEE *eats and eats.*

LEE *(mouth full of food)* Fucking starving.

Some time.

Have you seen her? Have you been in?

ARTHUR *shakes his head.*

Told me to wait. One of the nurses, she said, why don't you just have a seat downstairs.

Are you gonna see her?

No response.

Dad. Are you gonna?

ARTHUR *nods a little.*

Y'are?

ARTHUR Yes.

LEE Can I come with you?

ARTHUR What?

LEE When you go in, to see her. Can I come with you?

ARTHUR *nods a little.*

ARTHUR Yeah.

They eat.

LEE Pretty scared. D'you reckon she's gonna be alright?

No response.

Dad. D'you reckon she's gonna—

ARTHUR No idea. Eat y'tea Lee.

Beat.

LEE D'you love her?

ARTHUR *looks at* LEE.

Mum. D'you—

ARTHUR Just eat y'fucking tea.

LEE *cries.*

ARTHUR *tries to ignore, eats.*

LEE *continues crying.*

Fuck's sake what's the matter with ya?

LEE I don't wanna have to say goodbye.

ARTHUR What y'talking about?

LEE If she's not alright. Don't wanna have to—

ARTHUR Look come on. Come on.

LEE *continues crying.*

Never knew my mum y'know.

ARTHUR *waits for a response from* LEE.

LEE *subsides a little, wipes his eyes.*

LEE What?

ARTHUR My mum, never knew her.

LEE Why not?

ARTHUR Died.

LEE When?

DECEMBER, 1979.

ARTHUR When I was younger.

LEE Younger than me?

ARTHUR Yeah.

LEE wipes his eyes.

LEE Was it awful?

ARTHUR shrugs.

Were you sad?

ARTHUR Yeah. Course.

LEE Will you come here please?

ARTHUR stands, moves to LEE and hugs him.

Enter MELISSA, nine. MELISSA wears an astronaut's helmet.

ARTHUR puts down LEE, turns to MELISSA.

ARTHUR Hello lovely. Where've you been?

No response.

Tea's ready. Sausage and chips. D'you wanna come and sit down and have some tea with me and y'brother?

No response.

(meaning astronaut's helmet) D'you wanna take that off?

No response.

ARTHUR moves toward MELISSA.

Why don't we take it off?

MELISSA moves away from ARTHUR.

Wanna keep it on?

MELISSA nods a little.

You wanna keep it on?

MELISSA *nods a little.*

How y'gonna eat y'tea?

No response.

Lovely. How y'gonna.

(adopts ropey American accent) Viking 1 this is NASA speaking. Permission to come aboard Viking 1?

No response.

(accent) Viking 1 this is NASA, do you read, come in?

ARTHUR *waits for a response.*

(accent) Viking 1 this is NASA, do you read?

MELISSA Viking 1.

ARTHUR *(accent)* Viking 1, permission to come aboard?

MELISSA Permission granted.

ARTHUR *moves to* **MELISSA** *and picks her up.*

ARTHUR Why don't we take this off? Come and eat y'tea.

MELISSA No!

ARTHUR *watches* **MELISSA**.

ARTHUR Suit y'self.

ARTHUR *puts* **MELISSA** *down.*

ARTHUR *moves back to table and continues eating.*

MELISSA *cries, though not necessarily audibly.*

LEE Dad.

No response.

Dad Lis is crying.

No response.

Dad she's crying.

ARTHUR Eat y'tea.

LEE *moves to* **MELISSA**.

LEE Lis why don't you come and sit down? Dad's bought sausage and chips.

No response.

Lis.

MELISSA Fuck off Lee.

LEE How you gonna watch the fireworks? If you don't take y'helmet off, how you gonna watch the fireworks?

LEE *moves to the table, collects his food and moves back to* **MELISSA**.

Give you my sausage if you take y'helmet off?

No response.

That's two sausages Lis.

No response.

No?

LEE *moves to go back to his seat.*

MELISSA Wait wait wait wait.

LEE *stops.*

Promise you'll give me your sausage?

LEE Promise.

MELISSA *removes the astronaut's helmet.*

Beat.

MELISSA Give it then.

LEE *hands* MELISSA *his battered sausage.*

MELISSA *takes a giant bite.*

LEE *takes* MELISSA*'s hand and leads her to the table.*

All sit, all eat.

ARTHUR *sniffs, stands.*

LEE Where you going?

ARTHUR What?

LEE Where you going?

ARTHUR See y'mother.

LEE Can I come?

ARTHUR No.

LEE But you said?

ARTHUR Lee.

LEE You did! Minute ago, you said—

ARTHUR Not yet alright.

LEE Why not?

ARTHUR Because.

LEE What?

ARTHUR Because. One at a time.

LEE You're full o' shit.

ARTHUR I'm sorry?

    ARTHUR *watches* LEE. *No response.*

Gonna go and have a fag as well, so look after y'sister alright?

LEE What?

ARTHUR Might be a while's what I'm saying.

MELISSA Do you want y'chips?

ARTHUR Have 'em.

MELISSA Can I have a beer?

ARTHUR Beer's for grown ups.

MELISSA Lee's allowed one and he's not a grown up.

ARTHUR He's more of a grown up than you are sweetheart.

> **LEE** *sticks his tongue out at* **MELISSA**.

> **MELISSA** *gives* **LEE** *the finger.*

LEE Dad did you see what she just did?

> **ARTHUR** *puts a can of lager in both of his jacket pockets.*

That is so unfair. If I'd've don't that, you'd have given me a right—

ARTHUR Lee please! Eat y'tea. Both of you. No swearing. Alright?

No response.

Alright?

LEE *nods.*

ARTHUR *looks to* **MELISSA**.

You as well alright? Be nice to each other.

ARTHUR *moves to go.*

LEE Dad?

ARTHUR *stops:*

ARTHUR What?

LEE *shakes his head a little.*

Exit **ARTHUR**.

LEE You are such a little shit.

    MELISSA *stares at* LEE, *open mouthed.*

Who taught you the finger?

MELISSA Not saying.

LEE Was it Vicky Ward?

MELISSA Not saying.

LEE I'm gonna tell Dad.

MELISSA Tell him what?

    LEE *eats.*

    MELISSA *takes a can of lager and goes to open it.*

LEE What you doing?

No response.

He just said. Y'not allowed.

MELISSA So?

LEE So give it to me.

    MELISSA *shakes her head and holds on to the can of lager.*

Lis, please, just give it to me.

No response.

    LEE *goes to take the can,* MELISSA *holds onto it.*

    LEE *again goes to take the can,* MELISSA *again holds onto it.*

Brief tug of war.

    MELISSA *wins the tug of war, gets up, runs to the other side of the room and opens the can.*

Y'gonna be in so much shit.

MELISSA *drinks.*

MELISSA *instantly coughs and splutters, dropping the can to the floor.*

LEE *stands, moves toward* **MELISSA**.

You alright?

MELISSA *continues coughing.*

Lis you alright.

MELISSA *continues coughing.*

Dad! Dad!

Firework goes off outside.

LEE *and* **MELISSA** *look toward the window instantly.* **MELISSA** *stops coughing.*

You alright?

Another firework.

MELISSA *runs to the window.* **LEE** *follows her.*

LEE *looks at his watch.*

Well early.

Firework goes off. And another. And another. Etc.

The light from the fireworks glides across the faces of **LEE** *and* **MELISSA**.

Happy new year shithead.

MELISSA *sticks out her tongue and gives* **LEE** *the finger.*

You are gonna be in so much shit.

MELISSA *moves to* **LEE** *and hugs him.*

LEE *and* **MELISSA** *watch the fireworks.*

SEPTEMBER, 1985.

Bedroom. Evening.

House party. Music seeps through the floorboards.*

MELISSA, *fifteen, and* **RICHARD**, *fifteen.*

MELISSA *sits on the bed, head in hands, sobbing a little.* **RICHARD** *watches.*

RICHARD Are you alright?

No response.

There anything you want?

No response.

If it's any consolation, I don't think you're fat at all.

MELISSA What?

RICHARD Oh, hello.

MELISSA Fat?

RICHARD I just assumed—

MELISSA You what?

RICHARD ...

MELISSA Who are you?

RICHARD My name's Richard, hello.

---

* A licence to produce STARLINGS does not include a performance licence for any third-party or copyrighted music. Licensees should create an original composition or use music in the public domain. For further information, please see Music Use Note on page iii.

MELISSA Do we know each other?

RICHARD We go to the same school.

MELISSA Do I know you though?

RICHARD We were in the same group for maths for a bit, but then I got moved up.

MELISSA So why are you calling me fat?

RICHARD Wasn't.

MELISSA You weren't?

RICHARD No I mean I was saying, I was saying that, had somebody called you fat, in trying to guess what it is that's upset you, had somebody called you that, had somebody said—

MELISSA Yeah, I get it.

RICHARD I was just saying, you've no need to worry. In terms of—

MELISSA Yeah.

RICHARD Because you're not.

MELISSA Fat?

RICHARD *shakes his head.*

MELISSA *wipes her eyes.*

So what're you doin in here?

RICHARD I was just going to the toilet and I heard you. Through the door. Are you alright?

MELISSA You don't know then?

RICHARD ?

MELISSA Mean you don't know why I'm crying and that?

RICHARD *shakes his head a little.*

Don't know Sarah Green then?

RICHARD I know who she is, but. Not really.

MELISSA You reckon we go to the same school?

RICHARD We do, yeah.

MELISSA But we've never met each other?

RICHARD We were in the same—

MELISSA Same Maths group.

RICHARD Yeah, that's right. For a bit anyway.

Beat.

So what were they saying? Sarah Green and people, what were they saying?

MELISSA Not sure 's any of y'fucking business to be honest Richard.

RICHARD Oh. Sorry.

As along as everything's alright.

MELISSA Not really.

RICHARD Oh. Should we go and talk to them?

MELISSA You're fucking weird, d'you know that?

RICHARD Would you like me to go?

No response.

Don't normally come to these sorts of things.

MELISSA What?

RICHARD House parties. Don't normally come.

MELISSA Why'd y'come to this one then?

RICHARD My dad reckoned it'd be a good idea.

MELISSA Why's that?

RICHARD Says I don't have enough friends. Says at fifteen he had twice as many friends as I have.

MELISSA And how's it going, making friends?

RICHARD *considers, then:*

RICHARD Shit.

MELISSA *smiles a little.*

MELISSA Think you just need to relax. Have a few beers, get a bit pissed.

RICHARD I get really bad allergies.

MELISSA You what?

RICHARD Allergies. I get them really badly. Can't drink beer.

MELISSA Seriously?

RICHARD *nods.*

You drink anything?

RICHARD Sprits. Some spirits anyway. But the first time I ever drank vodka I got home really late and I accidentally took a shit on the bonnet of dad's car.

MELISSA You serious?

RICHARD *nods.*

RICHARD It was really bad. In the morning it was just sort of a bit hard. All the birds kept trying to eat it.

MELISSA *smiles.*

MELISSA D'you wanna sit down?

RICHARD *nods.*

RICHARD *moves to* **MELISSA** *and sits next to her on the bed.*

They were taking the piss out of me and my brother.

RICHARD How come?

MELISSA I live with my brother and m'nan. She's my aunt really but for some reason we've always called her Nan.

RICHARD Know what you mean. Woman lives a couple of doors down from us, got an in-growing toenail, Dad always calls her Nan, but I'm pretty certain we're not related at all.

MELISSA Anyway me and my brother're really close.

RICHARD *nods a little.*

Couldn't live without him really.

RICHARD What were they saying?

MELISSA Just stupid shit like we sleep together and stuff. And one of em said I look like fucking Thatcher.

RICHARD *looks at* MELISSA.

What?

RICHARD *shakes his head.*

Bet you a quid y'an only child?

RICHARD If I'm not?

MELISSA What?

RICHARD If I'm not, what do I get?

MELISSA You get a quid?

RICHARD Can't I have something else?

MELISSA What're you talking about?

RICHARD If you're wrong, and I'm not, can't I have something else? Don't really want a quid.

MELISSA What d'you want?

RICHARD *pauses.*

RICHARD Doesn't matter.

MELISSA No, go on.

RICHARD *is shaking his head.*

Go on, what was it?

RICHARD How did you know I was an only child?

MELISSA *shrugs.*

MELISSA Just you y'mum and y'dad then is it?

RICHARD Just me and dad.

MELISSA What happened to y'mum?

No response.

RICHARD Did you see Live Aid?

MELISSA What?

RICHARD Live Aid. It was a concert to raise money for starving children in Ethiopia.

MELISSA Yeah I know what was, just didn't hear what you said.

RICHARD Did you see it then?

MELISSA Yeah. Some of it.

RICHARD Do you like Queen?

MELISSA What?

RICHARD Queen, do you like them?

MELISSA Sort of.

RICHARD *sings a song in the style of a Queen song**

RICHARD *gets more and more into it.*

MELISSA *laughs.*

RICHARD *finishes the song.*

---

* A licence to produce STARLINGS does not include a performance licence for any third-party or copyrighted music. Licensees should create an original composition or use music in the public domain. For further information, please see Music Use Note on page iii.

What're you on?

Beat.

RICHARD I wasn't walking past the door.

MELISSA What?

RICHARD I saw you going upstairs.

RICHARD *pauses.*

Sort of came upstairs to ask you out.

A new song comes on downstairs, seeping through the floorboards.*

Beat.

You seen the video to this?

No response.

(*He's referring to a well-known A-ha video*) It's sort of animated, but sort of not. It's called Rotoscoping. It's where you film people normally and then later on you draw all over them. It's really good. Reckon eventually there won't be any point in having actors. Reckon it'll all just be drawn.

MELISSA *is smiling.*

MELISSA *moves to* **RICHARD**, *close.*

MELISSA *kisses* **RICHARD**.

They separate.

RICHARD *suddenly kisses* **MELISSA**. *It is a bit too hard, clumsy.*

---

* A licence to produce STARLINGS does not include a performance licence for any third-party or copyrighted music. Licensees should create an original composition or use music in the public domain. For further information, please see Music Use Note on page iii.

They separate.

MELISSA Have to do it softer.

RICHARD Sorry.

MELISSA You ever kissed anyone before?

RICHARD Just Nan.

MELISSA Have to shut your eyes.

> **RICHARD** *nods and shuts his eyes.*

And you have to get really close until you can almost feel each other. See how you can tell I'm really close even though we're not actually touching?

> **RICHARD** *nods a little.*

And then all you do is you just let your lips touch each other. Shouldn't even really have to move.

> **MELISSA** *kisses* **RICHARD**. *It is soft, slow.*

They separate.

See?

> **RICHARD** *nods.*

D'you wanna get into bed?

RICHARD ...

> **MELISSA** *moves to the bed and gets in.*
>
> **MELISSA** *removes her top and now wears only her bra.*

MELISSA You alright?

> **RICHARD** *nods and moves to the bed.*
>
> **RICHARD** *goes to get into the bed:*

Take off y'trousers.

RICHARD *looks at* **MELISSA**.

Go on.

RICHARD *hurriedly removes his trousers.*

RICHARD's *trousers get stuck around his shoes.*

RICHARD *flings his shoes off across the room and removes his trousers.*

RICHARD *gets into the bed.*

RICHARD It was a kiss. That was what I wanted. In the bet? I didn't want a quid I wanted a kiss.

MELISSA *kisses* **RICHARD**.

The kiss intensifies.

RICHARD *isn't quite sure where to put his hands.*

They separate.

MELISSA *goes under the duvet.*

RICHARD *shifts.*

MELISSA *begins giving* **RICHARD** *a blowjob.*

RICHARD *shifts, in a little pain.*

MELISSA *comes out from under the duvet suddenly.*

MELISSA You alright?

RICHARD *nods.*

Stop fucking moving about then.

MELISSA *goes under the duvet.*

MELISSA *resumes giving* **RICHARD** *a blowjob.*

RICHARD Wait. Wait, stop. Please, please, please.

MELISSA *(under duvet)* Fucking hell.

> **MELISSA** *comes out from under the duvet, wipes her mouth, lies back and catches her breath.*
>
> **RICHARD** *stands, begins putting on his trousers.*

What you doing?

RICHARD I'm sorry.

MELISSA What?

RICHARD I'm sorry.

MELISSA 'bout what?

RICHARD I better go.

MELISSA What?

> **RICHARD** *begins looking for his shoes.*

What're y'doing? Why y'going?

> **RICHARD** *puts on his shoes and moves to go.*

What're you doing?

> **RICHARD** *stops.*
>
> **RICHARD** *pauses.*

RICHARD She died. Giving birth. Dad says it was nothing to do with me. But.

MELISSA Are you alright?

RICHARD I'm sorry.

MELISSA Stop apologising. Sit down.

> **RICHARD** *does so.*

I'm sorry. About y'mum.

> **RICHARD** *nods a little.*

RICHARD Thanks. James Clarke told me your mum jumped out of her bedroom window. Is that true?

MELISSA gets out of bed and puts her top back on.

I'm sorry. You know whales when they cum, it's about twenty tonnes.

No response.

I mean. Good thing I'm not a whale, otherwise you'd've probably.

No response.

I'm sorry about what I said about your mum. I'm sorry.

MELISSA Who the fuck is James Clarke?

RICHARD He's in top set maths.

MELISSA Should keep his fucking mouth shut.

RICHARD I know, I'm sorry. I should go.

MELISSA Don't go, just stop saying stupid fucking stuff.

MELISSA pauses.

You know he's got AIDS don't you?

RICHARD …

MELISSA Freddie Mercury, you know he's got AIDS?

RICHARD shakes his head a little.

It was after gran died. Her and mum were really close. And then when dad went on strike he lost his job. Used to be a lorry driver. She was just really unhappy.

RICHARD What does your dad do now?

MELISSA shrugs.

MELISSA Left.

RICHARD Have you seen *Back To The Future* yet?

MELISSA *shakes her head a little.*

Do you wanna go? Could go next Tuesday if you're free? Or Wednesday. Or Thursday. Can't do Friday though, got Kung-Fu.

MELISSA Kung-Fu?

RICHARD *nods.*

You do Kung-Fu?

RICHARD Blue belt.

RICHARD *does a very brief move.*

MELISSA *laughs.*

RICHARD *bows.*

So what d'you reckon? Wanna see *Back To The Future* or what?

MAY, 1991.

MELISSA's *bedroom. Day.*

MELISSA, *twenty one, and* ARTHUR, *Forty three.*

At MELISSA's *feet, are a number of shopping bags (she has just returned home).*

ARTHUR *has with him a small holdall.*

MELISSA I don't understand, she just let you in?

ARTHUR Yeah.

MELISSA Who did you say you were?

ARTHUR Y'dad.

MELISSA And she just let you in?

ARTHUR Yeah.

Beat.

(re: shopping bags) Anything nice?

MELISSA *looks at* ARTHUR.

Shopping. Anything nice?

MELISSA 's just food. Mostly. Some socks.

ARTHUR Oh yeah. What sorta socks?

MELISSA What're you doing here?

ARTHUR Well. Passing through. Thought I'd stop by and—

MELISSA "Passing through"?

ARTHUR Yeah.

MELISSA Where're you passing through to?

ARTHUR ...

MELISSA If you're passing through, where is it you're passing through to?

>ARTHUR *hesitates.*

ARTHUR I'm not. Made that up. Come to see you. Say happy birthday.

MELISSA Birthday was two weeks ago.

ARTHUR What?

MELISSA My birthday. It was two weeks ago.

ARTHUR No?

>MELISSA *nods.*

I'm sorry.

MELISSA Are you?

ARTHUR I thought it was today.

>*No response.*

I thought we could go out.

MELISSA You thought we could go out?

>ARTHUR *nods.*

Where was it you thought we could go?

ARTHUR Planetarium.

>MELISSA *is taken aback by this, perhaps even a little moved, but she does her best not to reveal this to* ARTHUR.

Used to be into all that sort of stuff. Stars and that.

MELISSA Yeah, well, used to.

ARTHUR Don't fancy it then?

MELISSA Why're you really here?

ARTHUR I'm sorry. I know it's been a long time.

MELISSA You noticed?

ARTHUR Got a load of y'old letters in there.

MELISSA What?

ARTHUR YouR old letters. Keep 'em with me.

Silenced.

I've missed you.

MELISSA Fuck off.

Silence.

ARTHUR University and that then is it?

No response.

God knows where ya get it.

No response.

If you want me to go...

ARTHUR *watches* **MELISSA**.

MELISSA *shakes her head a little.*

Mind if I have a beer?

No response.

ARTHUR *reaches into his holdall, takes out a can of lager, opens it and drinks.*

ARTHUR *offers a can of lager to* **MELISSA**.

MELISSA No thank you.

ARTHUR *drinks.*

You look like shit you know.

ARTHUR Not looking too bad y'self.

MELISSA What d'you do?

>ARTHUR *reaches into the holdall and takes out a badly wrapped present.*

>ARTHUR *holds out the present for* MELISSA *to take.*

What is it?

>ARTHUR *gestures for* MELISSA *to take it.*

>MELISSA *takes the present.*

This is shit you know that don't you? Means nothing.

>ARTHUR *nods a little, sips his lager.*

>MELISSA *holds the present but resists opening it.*

Lee's birthday in a couple of months, you gonna be about for that one as well?

ARTHUR Hope so. Hoping to be about. Generally.

MELISSA Coming back then?

>ARTHUR *nods.*

Where you gonna stay? Can't stay with Nan. Lee's still there you know.

ARTHUR I know.

MELISSA Still lives at home.

ARTHUR I know.

MELISSA Wonder if he's ever gonna fucking move out.

ARTHUR Doing alright for himself though?

MELISSA Yeah. Works hard.

>*Beat.*

Where you gonna stay then?

ARTHUR Not sure t'be honest with you.

MELISSA Can't stay here.

ARTHUR Not expecting—

MELISSA You know I hardly talk about you. Used to. At first. Whenever I meet people now though, just tell 'em my parents are dead.

ARTHUR It's a pager.

MELISSA ...

ARTHUR Just clip it to y'waist and whenever anyone wants to get in touch with ya—

MELISSA I know what a pager is.

ARTHUR Gonna be big they reckon. Mostly doctors use 'em at the moment. Give it a year or two though, reckon they'll be everywhere.

MELISSA Why do I need a pager?

ARTHUR Keep in touch.

MELISSA Already tried that.

> **MELISSA** *holds out the present for* **ARTHUR**, *returning it.*

ARTHUR Least open it.

MELISSA I don't need it.

ARTHUR There's one for y'brother as well. Least have a think about it.

> **MELISSA** *holds onto the present.*

MELISSA How can you still drink that shit? Insides must be rotten.

ARTHUR Don't wanna go out then?

MELISSA *(meaning shopping)* Should put some of this in the fridge.

ARTHUR Wait.

MELISSA looks at **ARTHUR**.

MELISSA picks up most of the shopping bags and exits.

ARTHUR *suddenly moves to* **MELISSA**'s *handbag, which she has left on the floor.*

ARTHUR *opens the handbag and rummages through it.*

ARTHUR *takes out* **MELISSA**'s *purse and empties it.*

ARTHUR *puts the purse back and returns the handbag to its original state.*

ARTHUR *moves about the room, looking.*

ARTHUR *lifts up a number of small boxes, looks inside some of them.*

ARTHUR *finds a container that is full of small change.*

ARTHUR *empties the container into his jacket pocket.*

ARTHUR *finishes his lager, opens another and drinks.*

Re-enter **MELISSA**.

MELISSA *keeps her distance.*

English then is it?

No response.

Studying. Y'nan reckoned it was—

MELISSA I'm studying history.

ARTHUR *shuts his eyes, screws up his face, genuinely frustrated with himself for getting this wrong.*

ARTHUR What sorta history?

MELISSA What?

ARTHUR What sorta history is it y'studying?

MELISSA *pauses, watching* ARTHUR.

MELISSA It's all of it.

ARTHUR Right.

MELISSA I mean you choose your modules.

ARTHUR Sure.

MELISSA But the choice is across all of it.

ARTHUR Which ones you gonna choose then?

MELISSA Chosen.

ARTHUR …

MELISSA This is my final year.

ARTHUR No?

MELISSA *nods a little.*

Fuck me 's gone by. Go on then, which ones you go for?

MELISSA Why d'you wanna know?

ARTHUR Interested.

MELISSA Are you?

ARTHUR Course.

MELISSA What if I said it's none of your fucking business?

No response.

First year was just a bit of a general introduction. Second year it varied. Did a bit of Second World War, then a bit of French Wars of Religion. Now I'm doing Middle East.

ARTHUR Saddam and that is it?

MELISSA A bit, yeah.

ARTHUR What d'you make of all that then? Us going in and that?

MELISSA I think it's far more complicated than either you or I could ever imagine.

ARTHUR *nods a little.*

ARTHUR Should've known you were into all this.

ARTHUR *reaches into his holdall, rummages, and takes out a newspaper cutting.*

ARTHUR *hands the cutting to* MELISSA.

MELISSA *takes the cutting.*

Couldn't believe it when I saw that. Recognised you straight away.

MELISSA *looks at* ARTHUR, *then at the cutting.*

Looks mad.

MELISSA Was.

ARTHUR Poor old Maggie, eh?

MELISSA Poor old Maggie?

ARTHUR Rather her than old John boy.

MELISSA Poll-tax is one of the most ridiculous things I've ever heard of. Both as bad as each other.

ARTHUR *(re: newspaper cutting)* What was it like?

MELISSA Yeah. 'mazing.

ARTHUR No trouble?

MELISSA *shakes her head a little.*

Two hundred thousand people they reckoned.

MELISSA *nods a little and hands the cutting back to* ARTHUR.

ARTHUR *returns the cutting to his holdall.*

How's the fella?

MELISSA *looks at* **ARTHUR**.

Y'nan mentioned it. Last time I spoke to her. Wass his name? Robert something?

MELISSA Richard.

ARTHUR Richard, that's it. How is he?

MELISSA He's fine.

ARTHUR Wass he up to then?

MELISSA Look what're y'doing here?

ARTHUR *nods a little.*

Cos it's gonna take more than a pager. Gonna take more than a couple of. Newspaper articles.

ARTHUR I know.

MELISSA Mean I don't know where to begin.

ARTHUR *is nodding.*

Did you know you were always gonna go?

ARTHUR *sniffs, rubs his nose.*

ARTHUR *shakes his head.*

Just suddenly hit you did it?

ARTHUR *nods.*

It did?

ARTHUR Yeah.

MELISSA And that was it was it? Just got in the car and just.

ARTHUR Yeah.

MELISSA And in between?

ARTHUR What?

MELISSA In between, didn't think about getting in touch?

ARTHUR Course.

MELISSA Ten years is a long time. Over ten years.

ARTHUR I know.

MELISSA 's a really long time.

> ARTHUR *finishes his lager.*

> ARTHUR *takes out a packet of cigarettes and a box of matches.*

ARTHUR *(meaning smoking)* D'you mind?

MELISSA Do actually.

> ARTHUR *puts cigarettes and matches away.*

ARTHUR Y'been to y'brother's restaurant then?

MELISSA It's not really *his* restaurant.

ARTHUR Tried the food and that though?

MELISSA Yeah.

ARTHUR And?

MELISSA Yeah it's lovely. Got a real flair for it.

> MELISSA *cries suddenly.*

> ARTHUR *stands.*

> MELISSA *pulls herself together, moves away from* ARTHUR.

ARTHUR Sure you don't want a beer?

MELISSA I think you should go.

ARTHUR Didn't wanna try the planetarium?

MELISSA *stops herself from crying again.*

MELISSA Why're you doing this?

ARTHUR *hesitates.*

Where have you been?

ARTHUR Manchester, up North. Got a mate on the markets, been helping me out.

MELISSA Doing what?

ARTHUR Just selling and that.

MELISSA I don't believe you. I don't believe you.

ARTHUR It's the truth.

MELISSA Market, that's all you've been doing?

ARTHUR Couple of other bits and pieces, but, yeah.

MELISSA And what're you gonna do down here?

ARTHUR Well. Hoping to get a bit of money together. Got a mate, Marcus, big into communications and that. Hoping to get a bit of money together and have a think about starting up a little—

MELISSA Money?

ARTHUR For the business, yeah.

MELISSA Y'just want money?

ARTHUR You what?

MELISSA Money, that's what you're saying, that's why you've come back?

ARTHUR Not from you. Not from you love. Banks and that init.

MELISSA I'd like you to go now please.

ARTHUR Love.

No response.

ARTHUR *finishes his beer.*

ARTHUR *zips up his holdall.*

ARTHUR *takes a piece of paper from his pocket and writes a number on it.*

ARTHUR *holds out the piece of paper.*

That's me pager. Change y'mind about the planetarium.

MELISSA *doesn't take the piece of paper.*

ARTHUR *places the piece of paper on the bedside table.*

I'm not asking ya to forgive us.

ARTHUR *watches* **MELISSA**.

Exit **ARTHUR**.

MELISSA *sits.*

MELISSA *opens the present.*

MELISSA *opens the box and takes out the pager.*

MELISSA *looks at the pager.*

MELISSA *puts the pager back into the box.*

JUNE, 1993.

Honeymoon suite. Day.

Enter **MELISSA**, *twenty three,* **RICHARD**, *twenty three, and* **ARTHUR**, *forty five.* **MELISSA** *and* **RICHARD** *are holding* **ARTHUR** *up, his arms around their shoulders.* **ARTHUR** *looks unconscious.*

MELISSA *wears a wedding dress and* **RICHARD** *a suit.*

MELISSA *and* **RICHARD** *put* **ARTHUR** *down into a chair during the following:*

MELISSA He *hit* you?

RICHARD Not literally.

MELISSA What?

RICHARD I'd no idea who he was.

MELISSA ...

RICHARD It was just a reaction. I just. Reacted.

MELISSA It's fine.

RICHARD I'm sorry. Looks nothing like any of the photos you've shown me. You alright?

MELISSA *nods a little.*

MELISSA Why don't you go and get a plate of food from downstairs? Do you mind? Bring it up here. I'll get him some water.

RICHARD When was the last time you saw him?

No response.

MELISSA D'you mind telling Lee as well?

RICHARD Course.

> **RICHARD** *kisses* **MELISSA**.
>
> *Exit* **RICHARD**.
>
> *Exit* **MELISSA** *to bathroom.*
>
> **ARTHUR** *rouses a little, groans perhaps.*
>
> *Enter* **MELISSA** *with a glass of water and a hand towel.*
>
> **MELISSA** *kneels down in front of* **ARTHUR**.
>
> **MELISSA** *watches* **ARTHUR**.

ARTHUR Hello angel.

MELISSA You stink. You know that don't you? Not just booze. B.O.

ARTHUR You on the other hand.

MELISSA Drink this.

> **ARTHUR** *waves her off.*
>
> Drink it.
>
> **ARTHUR** *takes the glass and sips the water.*

ARTHUR Sorry I'm late. How's it all going?

MELISSA Why don't you take your jacket off?

> *No response.*
>
> Come on.
>
> **MELISSA** *helps* **ARTHUR** *to his feet and removes his jacket.*

ARTHUR Where is he then?

MELISSA Who?

ARTHUR The chap. The fella.

MELISSA Getting you some food.

ARTHUR How are ya?

MELISSA I'm fine.

ARTHUR Missed it then have I?

> MELISSA *nods*.

Meant to be a surprise. Bunch of flowers for ya somewhere.

MELISSA D'you know what time it is?

ARTHUR Know who you look like?

> *No response.*

Know who you look like don't ya?

> *No response.*

Look just like y'mum.

MELISSA Alright.

ARTHUR No word of a lie.

MELISSA Arthur d'you know what time it is?

ARTHUR No bad thing mind. She was beautiful. Absolutely beautiful.

> ARTHUR *looks at* MELISSA.

How are ya lovely?

> MELISSA *nods*.

Looking after ya is he?

> MELISSA *nods*.

Wass his name again?

MELISSA Richard.

ARTHUR Richard. Richard. Ordinary sort of name really.

MELISSA *hands* ARTHUR *the glass of water.*

ARTHUR *sips.*

MELISSA Are you alright?

ARTHUR *shrugs, sips water.*

You look ill. You listening? You don't look well.

ARTHUR I'm alright. You on the other hand.

MELISSA Where've you been?

ARTHUR *shrugs a little, sniffs.*

ARTHUR Not got you a present I'm afraid.

No response.

Old purse strings've been a bit.

ARTHUR *watches* MELISSA.

Look amazing.

MELISSA *moves away.*

What? What? 's true! You do. No wonder he's fucking laying me out. How old is he?

MELISSA We're the same age.

ARTHUR *doesn't know what that figure is.*

You should know how old I am. I'm not going to tell you.

ARTHUR How's the course?

MELISSA What?

ARTHUR The course, studying and that, how's it all going?

No response.

ARTHUR *pauses.*

Look I'm sorry. I am. Been a cunt. But I'm here, I'm here and I'm saying. I'm saying. Sorry. I'm. Sorry.

No response.

Love. Love.

Enter **RICHARD** *with a plate full of nibbles (sausage rolls, vol-au-vents, etc).*

RICHARD *moves to* **ARTHUR** *and hands him the plate of nibbles.*

ARTHUR Ta. (**ARTHUR** *holds out a hand for shaking*) Arthur by the way.

RICHARD Hi, yeah, Richard.

ARTHUR Nice to meet ya.

RICHARD Sorry about—

ARTHUR Don't worry about it.

RICHARD *nods.*

(meaning **MELISSA***)* Beautiful eh?

RICHARD Yeah.

ARTHUR You're a lucky bloke.

RICHARD I know.

ARTHUR What d'you do then Richard?

RICHARD Well it's a bit complicated.

ARTHUR Try me.

RICHARD I work in computers.

ARTHUR I know computers.

RICHARD Do you know much about the internet?

ARTHUR *nods a little.*

I, well, without going into it too much, I work for a small design company and I specialise in web sites. Have you seen many web sites?

ARTHUR Yeah yeah yeah yeah yeah.

RICHARD No idea whether it's going to take off. But. Enjoying it.

RICHARD *looks to* **MELISSA,** **MELISSA** *nods a little.*

ARTHUR Clever one this one eh?

Beat.

Well look thanks for getting in touch with us about all this.

RICHARD *nods a little.*

There're a loo in this place?

MELISSA Through there.

Exit **ARTHUR.**

RICHARD Are you alright?

MELISSA *nods a little.*

Do you want me to ask him to leave?

MELISSA It's fine.

RICHARD Sure?

MELISSA *nods.*

Toilet sounds offstage.

Enter **ARTHUR.**

ARTHUR Nice loo that. This it then is it?

MELISSA What d'you mean?

ARTHUR First night and that. This the place is it?

MELISSA Yeah.

ARTHUR Nice.

MELISSA Yeah.

ARTHUR When's the honeymoon?

RICHARD Not sure about that yet.

ARTHUR Not sure about the honeymoon?

RICHARD Money. You know.

ARTHUR Gotta have a honeymoon though.

RICHARD Oh no we will. We are going to. Just nothing's set in stone yet. All been a bit of a whirlwind.

ARTHUR Right.

RICHARD Because of the—

MELISSA Richard.

RICHARD It's alright. Aunt's told him.

ARTHUR Told me what?

RICHARD Angela told you didn't she?

ARTHUR *(to* **MELISSA***)* Wass he on about?

MELISSA Richard it's fine.

RICHARD No but she told me she'd told you.

Enter **LEE**, *25.* **LEE** *wears a suit.*

ARTHUR Here he is look.

LEE Everything alright? 's he pissed? Are you pissed?

MELISSA It's fine. *(To* **RICHARD***)* Why don't we go back downstairs?

RICHARD *(to* **ARTHUR***)* Lovely to meet you.

Arthur and Richard shake hands.

Exit **RICHARD** *and* **MELISSA**.

LEE Where were you then?

No response.

S'pose to be here hours ago.

No response.

Missed it. Know that don't ya? Whole thing, gone. Where's the phone?

No response.

The present, the phone, where is it?

No response.

Fuck's sake. Got her nothing then?

LEE *removes a pager clipped to his waist.*

LEE *chucks the pager to* ARTHUR. ARTHUR *doesn't catch it, pager falls to the floor.*

Waste of fucking money. D'you even know the fucking number?

ARTHUR I'm sorry.

LEE Are ya?

ARTHUR Yes.

LEE Sorry enough to turn up on time, sorry enough to remember the fucking present y'said y'd remember?

No response.

What happened to the planetarium? Where were ya?

No response.

She was fucking devastated about that y'know. 's not on.

ARTHUR I know.

LEE Pardon?

ARTHUR I know.

Silence.

Hear you're doing alright for y'self then?

No response.

Y'nan reckoned y'd had a couple of reviews and that?

No response.

Four stars she said.

No response.

Proud of ya.

LEE Fuck off.

ARTHUR Serious. Both of ya. Think about what I did. You're a fucking example.

LEE Think you better head off. She's under enough stress as it is.

ARTHUR *nods a little.*

ARTHUR Mind sending her back up?

LEE *moves to go.*

Thanks for inviting us.

LEE Wasn't up to me.

Exit **LEE**.

ARTHUR *alone.*

Enter **MELISSA**.

ARTHUR Gonna shoot off.

MELISSA You don't have to go.

ARTHUR *looks at* **MELISSA**.

You don't have to go. If you don't want to. You can stay.

ARTHUR *nods.*

Are you alright? I mean are you coping?

ARTHUR *nods.*

Have you been working?

ARTHUR *nods.*

You have?

ARTHUR On and off.

MELISSA What does that mean?

ARTHUR I mean it y'know. 'bout how y'look.

MELISSA If you're going to go again and not come back for a while, can you at least be honest with me and tell me now? Just makes dealing with it easier.

ARTHUR Gets hard. Because I don't know what I'm doing.

MELISSA Why don't you just stay?

ARTHUR ...

MELISSA It was my idea y'know. To invite you. Asked Richard to ask Nan to ask you. Thought there'd be more chance of you coming if you thought it was a surprise.

ARTHUR ...

MELISSA I think you should stay. Think you should speak to Richard, get to know him.

ARTHUR Let's have a dance.

MELISSA What?

ARTHUR Fucking married, least y'can do is have a dance w'ya old dad.

MELISSA There's no music.

Exit ARTHUR *toward bedroom/bathroom.*

Offstage, **ARTHUR** *tunes a radio. We hear various songs and radio stations being scanned through until* **ARTHUR** *settles upon something he likes, probably a ballad*.*

ARTHUR *turns up the volume as loud as it will go.*

Enter **ARTHUR**.

ARTHUR Little clock radio by y'bed.

ARTHUR *moves to* **MELISSA** *and takes her hand as if to begin a slow dance.*

ARTHUR *and* **MELISSA** *dance slowly and rhythmically, in circles.*

MELISSA *slowly smiles ever so slightly.*

Y'pregnant then?

MELISSA *looks at* **ARTHUR**.

MELISSA *nods a little.*

That's great. 's great. What y'gonna call it?

MELISSA Dunno.

ARTHUR Arthur if it's a bloke though?

MELISSA *smiles a little.*

Mean it y'know, look amazing.

ARTHUR *stops dancing, reaches into his pockets.*

Hold out y'hands.

MELISSA What?

ARTHUR Hands, hold em out.

---

* A licence to produce STARLINGS does not include a performance licence for any third-party or copyrighted music. Licensees should create an original composition or use music in the public domain. For further information, please see Music Use Note on page iii.

MELISSA holds out her hands.

Shut your eyes.

MELISSA hesitates.

ARTHUR gestures for MELISSA to shut her eyes.

MELISSA shuts her eyes.

ARTHUR shapes MELISSA's hands into a bowl shape.

ARTHUR reaches into his jacket pockets and takes out a handful of confetti from each.

ARTHUR places the confetti into MELISSA's hands.

Open.

MELISSA looks at the confetti, smiles.

Congratulations.

ARTHUR pecks MELISSA on the cheek.

MELISSA throws the confetti into the air and hugs ARTHUR.

MELISSA separates from ARTHUR, but remains close, running her hands gently over his face.

MELISSA Really don't look well y'know. Stay. We'll eat, have a drink. Please. Stay.

ARTHUR takes a step back from MELISSA, takes in the room.

ARTHUR nods.

You will?

ARTHUR Yeah.

MELISSA Promise?

ARTHUR ...

MELISSA D'you promise?

ARTHUR Yeah. Promise.

AUGUST, 1997.

MELISSA *and* RICHARD*'s bedroom. Day.*

MELISSA *sits on the end of the bed, watching television.* MELISSA *is watching a breaking news report on a car crash in Paris involving Princess Diana and Dodi Fayed. The volume on the television is low.*

RICHARD *is in bed, asleep.*

RICHARD *slowly rouses.*

MELISSA *turns off the television.*

RICHARD *yawns.*

MELISSA Didn't wake you did I?

RICHARD No.

MELISSA D'you want some breakfast?

RICHARD Should probably get packing.

MELISSA Be hungry though.

RICHARD Stop on the way. You alright?

MELISSA *nods.*

What were you watching?

MELISSA ...

RICHARD What? What is it?

MELISSA ...

RICHARD What?

MELISSA Been thinking about this holiday.

RICHARD Right.

MELISSA …

RICHARD What is it, what's the matter?

MELISSA …

RICHARD Lis?

>RICHARD *watches* MELISSA.

MELISSA I don't think I'm ready.

RICHARD What?

MELISSA Ready, I don't think I'm—

RICHARD To go on holiday?

>MELISSA *shakes her head.*

MELISSA To try again. Don't think I'm ready to—

RICHARD What? 's the Isle of Wight. Like the Isle of Wight.

>*No response.*

>Don't fancy it all then?

MELISSA I'm sorry.

RICHARD No, no.

>*Beat.*

>When you say you're not ready, d'you mean you're not ready at the moment? Or do you mean, at all, ever?

MELISSA …

RICHARD Lis.

MELISSA There was a woman in the paper who said she miscarried five times before she had her first child.

RICHARD …

MELISSA Just not sure I've got it in me.

RICHARD Course you have.

MELISSA No, but—

RICHARD No, listen to me, course you have.

> MELISSA *is shaking her head.*

Course you have, listen to me, course you have.

MELISSA Richard I'm sorry.

> *Silence.*

You should go.

RICHARD What?

MELISSA On y'own, you should go.

RICHARD Why would I wanna go to the Isle of Wight on my own? Wanna go with you. Wanna go with you.

> RICHARD *watches* MELISSA.

Are just talking about the holiday aren't we?

> *No response.*

Aren't we?

MELISSA I'm so sorry.

RICHARD What?

MELISSA I know this isn't what you want.

RICHARD What you talking about?

MELISSA In the long run.

RICHARD What?

MELISSA In the long run, I'm saying—

RICHARD Lis I don't know what's happened, I don't know what's going on, but you've gotta believe me.

MELISSA *shakes her head.*

You have, you have. You've gotta believe me.

MELISSA Say that now.

RICHARD Say that always.

MELISSA No but you say it now, but—

RICHARD Listen to me, listen to me. I'm telling you, I don't care if we never have children. I don't. And d'you know why, d'you know why I don't care?

No response.

RICHARD *watches* **MELISSA.**

What's changed, I don't understand?

No response.

RICHARD *moves to* **MELISSA,** *close.*

I love you. You listening to me?

MELISSA It's what you want.

RICHARD What?

MELISSA You've talked about it.

RICHARD Forget it.

MELISSA Richard please, you have. Talked about it for years.

RICHARD I've changed my mind.

MELISSA Please.

RICHARD No I have. You've changed yours, I've changed mine. Don't want 'em, fuck 'em.

Beat.

Lis if we're gonna call it a day, let's not call it a day because of something that's *not* happened. If that's really what we're gonna do, let's at least do it because of something that's. Something that's actually.

No response.

Lis. Lis look at me. You know I'll do whatever you want? Don't you? Need a bit of space, bit of time, fine. Just say it. I'm gone. If that's what it takes, fine, let's do it, 's just get on with it.

No response.

I don't know what I'll do. I don't know what I'll do.

MELISSA You'll be fine.

RICHARD *shakes his head.*

You will.

RICHARD *shakes his head.*

You will.

RICHARD Have I done something?

MELISSA No.

RICHARD Because if I have, if it's because of something that I've actually done, just—

MELISSA It's not.

RICHARD I know things have been a bit rough. Know they have. Know we've been. Rowing and—

MELISSA Richard.

RICHARD Just tell me! Tell me what it is. Because we can fix it.

MELISSA *shakes her head.*

No we can, we can, we can fix it. We can fix it.

MELISSA You deserve better.

RICHARD What?

MELISSA You do.

RICHARD Oh rubbish.

MELISSA And I can feel it, I can. Inside me, this. Can feel it, just.

RICHARD watches MELISSA.

RICHARD I don't understand?

No response.

I don't understand?

MELISSA I can't end up like her.

RICHARD What?

MELISSA Just can't.

RICHARD Who?

MELISSA And the thought of bringing a child, into that, makes me sick. Because it's not fair.

RICHARD Your mum y'mean?

No response.

You mean y'mum?

MELISSA When we row – And it's not often, it's not. It's not. But when we do, when we do, I'm back on the stairs and I'm peering through the railing.

RICHARD Lis, Lis, everyone gets worried about this sort of thing.

MELISSA shakes her head.

No, no, they do, they do. But you have to understand, have to realise: y'not like her, y'not. Listen to me, listen to me.

RICHARD moves toward MELISSA, MELISSA moves away.

Listen to me. We can call it a day for whatever you want. We can. But not for this. Not for this. Sort of stuff you worry about when y'kids. Not now. Not now.

RICHARD *moves toward* MELISSA, *close.*

RICHARD *kisses* MELISSA, *extraordinarily gently.*

They separate.

Why don't we start packing and see how we feel?

MELISSA *shakes her head.*

D'you feel different then, about me?

MELISSA No.

RICHARD You don't?

MELISSA No, never.

RICHARD *watches* MELISSA.

RICHARD I mean it y'know. I really don't mind.

Beat.

Could adopt. Mean if you really didn't wanna. Try again. Could do it that way, couldn't we? Couple of years' time. Couldn't we?

MELISSA *hugs* RICHARD.

What?

They separate.

MELISSA *holds* RICHARD's *face in her hands.*

What, what is it?

MELISSA *kisses* RICHARD *on the neck.*

Lis?

MELISSA *kisses* RICHARD *on the other side of his neck.*

Lis I don't understand, what's going on?

MELISSA *kisses* RICHARD *on the lips, soft.*

They separate.

What?

MELISSA *smiles every so slightly.*

What?

MELISSA *moves to go.*

Lis. Lis.

Exit **MELISSA**.

RICHARD *alone.*

RICHARD *moves.*

RICHARD *turns on the television. The news remains the same.*

RICHARD *changes the channel. The news remains the same.*

SEPTEMBER, 1999.

Village hall kitchen, small, cramped. Various crates of soft drinks, beers, etc.

Constant hum of conversation from the hall audible throughout.

ARTHUR, *fifty one, sits on a keg.* ARTHUR *wears a black suit, white shirt and black tie.*

ARTHUR *is rolling a cigarette.*

ARTHUR *lights the cigarette and begins smoking it.*

Enter MELISSA, *twenty nine.* MELISSA *wears black also.*

ARTHUR *stands on* MELISSA*'s entrance.*

ARTHUR *gestures for* MELISSA *to take a seat on the keg.*

No response.

ARTHUR *(meaning cigarette)* Don't mind do you?

MELISSA *shakes her head.*

I thought what you said was wonderful. I just wanted to thank you in private really. Why don't you sit down?

MELISSA *sits on a load of soft drink crates.*

Would you like a drink?

MELISSA *shakes her head.*

Something else to eat?

MELISSA No thank you.

> ARTHUR *watches* MELISSA.

ARTHUR Are you alright?

MELISSA ...

ARTHUR You've been really brave.

MELISSA What is it? What do you want to talk about?

ARTHUR Well. First thing I wanted to say was I thought what you said was lovely.

MELISSA You just did.

ARTHUR I know.

MELISSA Just told me that.

ARTHUR Second thing I wanted to say was thank you, for contacting me.

MELISSA You're the next of kin.

ARTHUR Still.

MELISSA Had to.

ARTHUR Still.

MELISSA If it'd been up to me.

> MELISSA *looks at* ARTHUR.

You look different.

ARTHUR Thanks.

MELISSA Didn't say better.

> ARTHUR *smiles a little.*

ARTHUR Look I wanted to invite you up to York for the millennium. You and Lee. Anyone else for that matter. Wanted to invite you up to my place.

MELISSA York?

ARTHUR *nods:*

ARTHUR 's where I've been living for the last—

MELISSA I know.

ARTHUR Right.

MELISSA Nan told us.

ARTHUR Right, course. Anyway I just wanted to get you alone to ask you. So ya know I'm serious.

MELISSA As opposed to what?

ARTHUR As opposed to. In the past when we've. And I may have.

MELISSA Spit it out.

ARTHUR *is sweating.*

ARTHUR *goes to one of the boxes of soft drinks, opens it, takes out a can of something fizzy, opens it, and drinks (and drinks and drinks).*

ARTHUR *loosens his tie.*

ARTHUR Melissa I'm sorry.

Silence.

Did you, did you hear what I—

MELISSA Yeah.

ARTHUR You did?

MELISSA Yeah you're sorry.

ARTHUR Really want you to know that though.

No response.

Been going to church.

MELISSA In York?

ARTHUR Yeah. Some of people I've met, they've—

MELISSA Not gonna try and convert me are ya?

ARTHUR What?

MELISSA Convert me.

ARTHUR No. Not saying I believe it. Just. Some of the people I've met, talking to 'em, really helped me think about. What it means. You and Lee. Everything I've put y'through.

MELISSA And what does it mean?

ARTHUR Well I don't know. No idea.

MELISSA Obviously haven't been that helpful then.

ARTHUR Alright "means" wasn't quite the right word.

MELISSA Clearly.

ARTHUR Stop being smart will ya.

Beat.

Sorry. I'm sorry. I'm not asking you to forgive me.

MELISSA Good.

ARTHUR All I'm asking is that you let me try and explain.

MELISSA No.

ARTHUR What?

MELISSA No.

ARTHUR If I said I wanted us to try and. What would you say?

No response.

Do you hate me?

MELISSA What?

ARTHUR Hate me.

No response.

I was sorry to hear about Richard.

MELISSA Were you.

ARTHUR Course. Want y'to be happy.

Silence.

Stopped drinking. Nearly six months.

Silence.

I don't know what to say?

MELISSA Neither do I.

ARTHUR Is it too late?

MELISSA What?

ARTHUR All this? 's it too late?

MELISSA I don't know.

ARTHUR Because if it's not, I'd love for us to be able to—

MELISSA What?

ARTHUR Saying. I'd love for us to be able to. See each other. A bit, bit more often.

MELISSA See each other?

ARTHUR Yeah.

MELISSA What would you like to do?

ARTHUR ...

Beat.

Keep thinking about all the things I wish I'd said to y'nan. And the idea of it happening to you lot, you and Lee, chokes me.

MELISSA Never slagged you off y'know. Was amazed. All the shit me and Lee used to say about you, never joined in.

ARTHUR *nods a little.*

Scared really aren't you?

ARTHUR What?

MELISSA Scared.

ARTHUR Yeah.

MELISSA Aren't you?

ARTHUR Yeah.

MELISSA Scared. Some people try for years t'have children you know.

ARTHUR Love.

MELISSA I've really tried to forget you. I have. But I can't.

    MELISSA *is trying not to cry.*

ARTHUR Love.

MELISSA Don't.

ARTHUR I'm sorry if I upset you.

MELISSA You do. You do upset me. You make me furious. You make me hate people. Scared of them. Richard. But, despite all that, in spite of it all, no matter how hard I try, I just can't. And I've tried. You wouldn't believe how hard I've tried. But I can't. Because you're my dad.

ARTHUR Love.

MELISSA Aren't you?

ARTHUR Yeah.

MELISSA Mean you are aren't you?

ARTHUR Love.

MELISSA You're my dad.

    ARTHUR *nods.*

    ARTHUR *moves toward* **MELISSA**.

ARTHUR Love.

MELISSA Thanks for coming Arthur.

ARTHUR What?

MELISSA Thanks for coming.

ARTHUR Hang on.

MELISSA Best of luck in York.

ARTHUR Wait, hang on.

> MELISSA *moves to go.*

Wait wait wait wait wait, come on.

No response.

Melissa. Melissa.

> ARTHUR *takes a hold of* MELISSA*'s arm.* MELISSA *instantly frees herself.*

MELISSA What ya doin? What d'you think y'doing?

ARTHUR I just want us to be able to—

MELISSA I don't care. D'you understand? I don't actually care.

ARTHUR Look.

MELISSA I asked you to stay, before, and I meant it, I meant it and you fucked off anyway.

ARTHUR I know.

MELISSA Even though you promised. Even though you said you would. Even though you talked to my friends, to Richard, even though you bought us drinks and ate all the food, you didn't actually do what I wanted you to do.

ARTHUR I know.

MELISSA You didn't actually do what you said you would.

ARTHUR I know.

MELISSA I'd like you to go.

ARTHUR …

MELISSA I'd like you to leave. And I don't mean here, I don't mean today, I mean leave, I mean go, and I mean don't come back. And if I see you again, I swear to God, I will wring your fucking neck.

Beat.

D'you understand?

ARTHUR Nothing I can say then?

No response.

ARTHUR *moves to go.*

Best o'luck in the new year.

Exit **ARTHUR**.

MELISSA *alone.*

MELISSA *moves. Stops.*

MELISSA *moves to one of the boxes of lager, rips it open, takes out a can, opens it and drinks. And drinks and drinks.*

MELISSA *sits on the same keg* **ARTHUR** *sat on earlier.*

MELISSA *looks at the can of lager.*

MELISSA *puts the can of lager down.*

SEPTEMBER, 2001.

RICHARD's *bedroom. Day.*

MELISSA, *thirty one, and* **RICHARD**, *thirty one.*

RICHARD Reminded me of that film, *Independence Day*? Did you ever see it?

MELISSA Yeah.

RICHARD Will Smith and Jeff Goldblum wasn't it?

MELISSA Used to quite fancy Jeff Golblum.

RICHARD No?

> **MELISSA** *nods.*

Jeff Goldblum.

Beat.

Watched it all live online.

MELISSA Glad I didn't see it.

RICHARD Awful to say, but it was just incredible. To watch.

MELISSA You know the same thing nearly happened in ninety-three?

RICHARD No? Really?

MELISSA They used a van though. Didn't quite work from what I understand.

RICHARD A van?

MELISSA Yeah they left it in the car park underneath. I think about six people died?

RICHARD Had no idea.

MELISSA Surprised they've not mentioned it yet. On the news.

RICHARD Yeah.

Silence.

MELISSA How are you?

RICHARD *nods a little.*

How's y'dad?

RICHARD Okay. I think. Okay.

MELISSA Should've let me know sooner.

RICHARD Didn't want to—

MELISSA I would have come round.

RICHARD It's been okay really.

MELISSA No but I would've.

RICHARD *nods.*

So what've they said?

RICHARD Not a lot really. Probably going to have to give up smoking. Not really mentioned drink, but I'd've thought he's gonna have to give that up as well.

MELISSA Were you in when it happened?

RICHARD Yeah. Yeah, I was. Wasn't what you'd expect to be honest. Whenever you see it on telly it's always people clutching at their chests and falling to their knees, but he just walked into my room and said, "can't feel my arms".

MELISSA What did you do?

RICHARD Just got him a glass of water and went back to bed. Hour later, same thing happened again, so I called an ambulance.

MELISSA *hugs* **RICHARD**.

It's alright.

MELISSA I love your dad.

RICHARD *ends the hug.*

RICHARD Was actually something else I wanted to talk to you about.

MELISSA Okay.

RICHARD Alright to talk about it?

MELISSA Don't know unless you tell me.

RICHARD *hesitates.*

RICHARD Was hoping we could talk about. Us, the house.

MELISSA *nods a little, takes this in.*

Been thinking about it a lot recently and now with Dad, just think it might be the right time to think about making it. Official.

MELISSA Official?

RICHARD *nods.*

RICHARD Not expecting you to have to do it. Solicitor's already looking into getting a contract drawn up. Not too bothered about all that really, more the house I'd like to get going on.

MELISSA The house?

RICHARD I know it sounds like a lot—

MELISSA No.

RICHARD But, with Dad being—

MELISSA It's fine.

RICHARD I'd quite like to go part-time, but I can't really afford to do that unless—

MELISSA It's fine.

RICHARD If there was any way of us being able to keep it and you staying there, you know I'd—

MELISSA I know.

RICHARD But I've thought about it and I just think now's a really good time to sell.

MELISSA It's fine. Honestly. 'bout time I got on with it anyway. Place is enormous.

RICHARD What d'you think you'll do then?

MELISSA Not sure really.

RICHARD But you'll be alright?

MELISSA Yeah. Course.

Silence.

RICHARD God this is strange. You know I remember the first time I met you.

MELISSA *nods.*

C'you remember?

MELISSA Yeah.

RICHARD Never told you this, but I'd fancied you for weeks.

MELISSA What?

RICHARD Honest to God. Followed you home once.

MELISSA What?

RICHARD Sounds awful when you say it like that. Obviously I wasn't gonna do anything.

MELISSA Followed me home.

RICHARD Just wanted to see your house, where you lived, where it was. Just wanted to know more about you.

MELISSA Remember telling you Freddie Mercury had AIDS and you looking at me like I'd given it to him.

SEPTEMBER, 2001.

RICHARD *and* MELISSA *smile.*

RICHARD You were the first girl I'd ever been with.

MELISSA It showed.

RICHARD First and last.

MELISSA Don't say things like that.

RICHARD What?

MELISSA Last.

RICHARD You know what I mean.

MELISSA Hate to think of you being unhappy.

RICHARD I'm not.

MELISSA Because of me though. Hate to think of you being unhappy because of—

RICHARD I'm not. Not at all.

MELISSA You were too good.

RICHARD It's alright.

MELISSA You were you were. Sounds ridiculous when you say it aloud, but you were.

RICHARD Think we know that's not true.

MELISSA *shakes her head.*

MELISSA *looks at* RICHARD.

…

MELISSA *kisses* RICHARD.

They separate.

Silence.

RICHARD *kisses* MELISSA.

RICHARD *breaks away suddenly, moves away from* **MELISSA**.

MELISSA What?

RICHARD *kisses* **MELISSA**.

RICHARD *breaks away suddenly, moves away from* **MELISSA**.

RICHARD Fuck!

MELISSA It's alright.

RICHARD 's not.

MELISSA It is, it's alright.

RICHARD It's not because I want it, I want it.

RICHARD *looks at* **MELISSA**.

I miss you. I have fucking missed you.

MELISSA *nods a little.*

It is though isn't it? How it feels isn't it?

MELISSA *nods.*

It's incredible, this pull. Stop yourself from acting on it, almost unbearable. 'mount of times I've gone round to the house, spare set of keys, 'mount of times I've gone round and thought about just opening the door and fucking, running up the stairs and screaming—

MELISSA I know.

RICHARD Isn't it though? Just incredible.

MELISSA Yeah.

RICHARD Don't think I've ever felt so convinced of anything in my entire life. I mean it's fine, it's absolutely fine, I completely understand that we're—

MELISSA Richard.

RICHARD No it is, I mean it is fine. Course it is, has to be. You wanted one thing, I wanted another: it's fine.

But sometimes—

MELISSA I know.

RICHARD Sometimes—

MELISSA I know.

RICHARD Sometimes you feel like. God you feel like—

MELISSA I know.

RICHARD Don't you?

MELISSA *nods.*

Don't you though, you feel like—

MELISSA Yeah.

RICHARD And seeing those people, those planes, that dust, you think, you think: that's what it is, that's how it feels. This fear. This deep, unbearable, uncontrollable fear. Isn't it though?

MELISSA *nods.*

You think: I am not letting you go. I am not letting you go ever. And that's what it's gonna take, that is what it is going to take to take you away from me. Isn't it?

Beat.

I fucking love you.

MELISSA *kisses* RICHARD.

MELISSA *and* RICHARD *kiss and kiss and kiss. Hard, intense kisses.*

MELISSA *and* RICHARD *fall onto the bed.*

MELISSA *and* RICHARD *begin kissing each other beyond just their lips.*

MELISSA and RICHARD begin fiercely undressing one another's trousers.

MELISSA and RICHARD begin to have sex.

MELISSA and RICHARD have sex.

RICHARD orgasms. The adrenalin subsides.

MELISSA and RICHARD catch their breath, steady their breathing.

You alright?

MELISSA Yeah. Yeah, you?

RICHARD Yeah.

RICHARD and MELISSA smile.

RICHARD and MELISSA begin to laugh, first a little then a lot.

Blimey. Sorry it wasn't very—

MELISSA It's fine.

RICHARD Been a while.

MELISSA It's fine.

MELISSA and RICHARD remain wrapped around one another for a moment or two.

RICHARD stands, fastens his trousers.

RICHARD We're alright about the house then?

MELISSA watches RICHARD.

Alright to go ahead?

MELISSA What?

RICHARD The house, don't mind if I start—

MELISSA The house?

RICHARD *nods.*

RICHARD What?

> MELISSA *shakes her head.*
>
> I don't understand, what is it, what's the matter?
>
> *Silence.*

MELISSA No you're right, sell it.

RICHARD What?

MELISSA You're right.

RICHARD I don't understand?

> *No response.*
>
> What is it, what's the matter?

MELISSA A moment ago you said it was unbearable?

RICHARD It is.

MELISSA Unbearable?

RICHARD Yes.

MELISSA And now?

RICHARD What?

MELISSA Now, is it unbearable now?

> RICHARD *hesitates.*

RICHARD I'm sorry but I don't understand what we're talking about?

> *No response.*
>
> MELISSA *readies herself to leave.*

MELISSA Give my love to y'dad.

RICHARD Wait, what?

MELISSA Your dad, give him my love won't you?

RICHARD Don't understand?

MELISSA Bye Richard.

RICHARD Have I upset you? Is that what it is, you upset about something?

No response.

Hadn't planned to fuck you you know?

MELISSA That's nice.

RICHARD You know what I mean. Wasn't some sort of—

MELISSA I know.

RICHARD No but do you? Because it seems like you're—

MELISSA I do know. I do.

RICHARD It is unbearable. I did mean that.

MELISSA I think you're actually a lot better off than you think.

RICHARD What?

MELISSA You know I saw you.

RICHARD What?

MELISSA Outside my house. I saw you. When you came up to me at that house party I just pretended I'd never met you because I was too embarrassed to admit that, actually. Actually.

MELISSA *is perhaps smiling a little.*

I hope we stay in touch—

RICHARD Lis.

MELISSA No I do I hope that we stay in touch.

RICHARD We will.

MELISSA But if we don't—

RICHARD We will though.

MELISSA If we don't though, I want you to know—

RICHARD What're you talking about?

MELISSA I want you to know that—

RICHARD Course we're gonna stay in touch, what you talking about?

No response.

Lis.

MELISSA Let me know if there's anything I can do to help with the house.

Exit MELISSA.

JANUARY, 2002.

Restaurant. Evening. Heavy rainfall throughout.

MELISSA, *thirty one, and* **LEE**, *thirty one.* **MELISSA** *is soaking wet.* **LEE** *wears his chef's whites and is holding a plate of food.*

Silence except for rainfall.

LEE Why don't we just start at the beginning?

MELISSA *sits at one of the tables.*

LEE *places down the plate of food in front of* **MELISSA**.

MELISSA Got anything to drink?

LEE *moves behind the bar and pours* **MELISSA** *a glass of tap water.*

LEE *returns to the table and places down the glass of tap water.*

Not got anything stronger?

LEE Just eat y'food.

MELISSA What is it?

LEE Fishcake. Salmon and watercress.

MELISSA *eats.*

MELISSA 's good. 's really good.

LEE I know.

MELISSA *eats.*

Come on then.

MELISSA What?

LEE Finish the story.

MELISSA He wants to sell the house. Needs the money to look after his dad.

LEE *exhales.*

(*mouthful of food*) Mm, and the other thing he wants, is a divorce. There was I thinking we were gonna have a bit of a. You know.

LEE *nods.*

There was I thinking it was gonna be a bit of a—

LEE Yeah.

MELISSA Only to discover that, actually—

LEE So how d'you get from that to fucking each other?

MELISSA What?

LEE Saying—

MELISSA Didn't just "fuck" each other.

LEE Know what I mean.

MELISSA Didn't just "fuck" each other.

LEE Just saying—

MELISSA Why would you say that?

LEE I'm just saying—

MELISSA I have come here, I have come here because I'm—

LEE I know.

MELISSA Because I'm petrified.

LEE Alright.

MELISSA I have come here, to see you, I have come here because—

LEE Alright, alright. Fuck's sake. Sorry. Been sweating m'tits off all day and all of a sudden y'come crashing in and—

MELISSA Can go if you want?

LEE Not what I'm saying.

MELISSA I can leave.

LEE Not fucking saying—

MELISSA I'll go, I'll go.

LEE Fuck's sake sit down will ya.

Silence except for rainfall.

I'm sorry. But I haven't heard from ya in weeks and suddenly y'at m'front door, dead o' night, wailing about having a fucking. Lot to take in.

LEE *takes* MELISSA*'s glass of water and drinks.*

Sorry about Richard. Nice bloke. But there's no point—

MELISSA What?

LEE Saying. Sounds like he's made up his mind.

MELISSA What?

LEE I'm only saying, no point in letting y'self—

MELISSA He's my husband.

LEE I know—

MELISSA My husband.

LEE I know but I'm just saying, sounds like he's made up his mind. And I know it's hard, but the best thing you can do now is just forget about it and start thinking about how y'gonna manage this other thing.

No response.

Lis. Lis will you look at me?

No response.

Will you look at me please?

MELISSA *does so.*

I'm sorry. Alright? I'm sorry. Because it sounds fucking awful, it does.

MELISSA S'pose to be today. S'pose to have had it done today. Nurse came and sat next to me and started explaining how it works. They have to stop the heart. That's the first thing they have to do. Have to stop its heart because I'm past fifteen weeks.

Beat.

Anyway I couldn't bear it. Left, went home. I don't want children Lee.

LEE Listen.

MELISSA I can't.

LEE I'll help ya.

MELISSA What?

LEE Saying, I'll help ya.

MELISSA What're you talking about?

LEE This place is doing alright, not exactly struggling for money, so I'm saying—

MELISSA Don't need any money. Don't need any money.

LEE Alright, okay, alright. What are y'gonna do then?

MELISSA Have to go back.

LEE What?

MELISSA Make another appointment.

LEE No.

MELISSA What?

LEE Not letting ya.

MELISSA ...

LEE Shoulda been more careful.

MELISSA Fuck off.

LEE 's true. Serious. And I'll tell ya this now, you go through with it, me and you.

LEE shakes his head.

Be it.

MELISSA Don't say that. Lee please. Don't say things like that.

No response.

What about my job?

Beat.

Mean I think about Mum, think about how unhappy she was and 's cos she never left the house, cos she never fucking did anything.

LEE Have to forget all that.

MELISSA I'm not gonna give up my job. I'm good at it. And I've worked hard, really hard.

LEE Fucked then is what y'saying? Isn't it? Fucked.

Silence except for rainfall.

MELISSA You know I look at where we are now and 's exactly where we were when I was at uni.

LEE What?

MELISSA Just goes in cycles. Abroad, here, you, dad. Spent years tryina escape it. Have. And all I'm saying is, all I'm saying is, sometimes the worst thing you can think of is the best thing to do.

LEE Lis.

MELISSA Listen to me.

LEE Y'scared, 's all it is. Just need to let go of it all. Who'd've thought, thirty years ago, who'd've thought I'd have me own restaurant, m'own business?

MELISSA No I know.

LEE When you fucked off to uni and I got a job peeling potatoes, people thought I was a right—

MELISSA No I know, I know, I know.

LEE Not saying 's easy, not saying 's not hard fucking work. But in the end—

MELISSA Why aren't you with anyone?

LEE What?

MELISSA Why aren't you with anyone?

LEE What you talking about?

MELISSA You live alone Lee. All these years. Least I tried.

Beat.

If I don't wanna be a mother, I don't have to. And maybe that's better, maybe it's better I'm not.

Beat.

Thanks for the fishcake. I'll see you later.

MELISSA *moves to go.*

LEE I'm not with anyone because.

MELISSA *stops.*

MELISSA What?

LEE Saying. Y'right. Have made a choice, just not the one you think it is.

MELISSA …

LEE If anything happened to you Lis, if something happened and I wasn't around, dunno what I'd fucking do?

MELISSA I don't need looking after.

LEE I know.

MELISSA I'm alright.

LEE I know, I know you are.

MELISSA Then I don't understand?

Silence except for rainfall.

LEE I'm not some fuck up. Got the restaurant. I'm alright.

MELISSA I know. I know.

LEE Got you.

MELISSA 's true. You do.

AUGUST, 2007.

Hospital canteen. Evening. A large window runs across the back of the canteen.

ARTHUR, *fifty nine, and* **LEE**, *thirty nine.* **ARTHUR** *has a holdall.*

ARTHUR Vodka?

LEE *nods.*

LEE Walking Lilly home from school, came in, shit everywhere. Gonna kill me for ringing ya y'know.

ARTHUR I'm glad you did.

LEE She's right though. What she told ya.

ARTHUR …

LEE To fuck off, she's right.

ARTHUR How's the restaurant?

LEE 's alright.

ARTHUR I'd like to come.

LEE …

ARTHUR To the restaurant, I'd like to book a table.

LEE Got Yellow Pages haven't ya?

Silence.

ARTHUR It's good to see you.

LEE Is it?

ARTHUR It is, yeah. How are you?

LEE *sniffs.*

There anything you need?

LEE What?

ARTHUR Need, anything ya—

LEE "Need"?

ARTHUR ...

LEE "Need", that what ya said?

ARTHUR *nods.*

Was it?

ARTHUR *nods.*

"Need".

LEE *laughs.*

ARTHUR Mean it.

No response.

On the email now if you wanna get in touch bit more often.

LEE Email?

ARTHUR Yeah 's uh, something something something dot co dot something-or-other. (ARTHUR *searches his pockets*) Got a card with it on here somewhere.

LEE Don't want ya fucking email.

ARTHUR *looks at* LEE. ARTHUR *gives up the search.*

'gainst my better judgement all this.

ARTHUR Like I said, grateful.

LEE Yeah. Well.

Beat.

's because o' you.

No response.

Know that don't ya?

No response.

Hello?

ARTHUR I've said I'm sorry.

LEE Have ya?

ARTHUR Yes.

LEE Oh well thass alright then.

ARTHUR Lee.

LEE Arthur.

Silence.

ARTHUR Is Lilly alright? It is Lilly isn't it?

LEE *nods.*

She's alright is she?

LEE *nods.*

LEE At a neighbour's.

ARTHUR Go and collect her if it'd help?

LEE She's alright.

ARTHUR How old is she?

No response.

LEE *takes out his wallet, takes out a small photograph.*

LEE *hands the photograph to* ARTHUR.

ARTHUR *looks at the photograph.*

She's beautiful.

ARTHUR *begins to cry, virtually silently.*

LEE What ya doin?

ARTHUR *tries to stop himself crying, can't.*

Stop it.

Can't.

Said stop it, wass the matter with ya?

Can't, sniffs.

LEE *takes the photograph back from* ARTHUR.

LEE *takes some tissue from his pocket and hands it to* ARTHUR.

Here.

ARTHUR *takes the tissue, wipes his eyes, blows his nose, etc.*

Shouldn't be letting ya get away with all this. Should be you worrying about us.

Enter MELISSA, *thirty seven.* MELISSA *wears hospital pyjamas and has bandages around both wrists.*

ARTHUR *blows his nose again.*

MELISSA Got a cold?

LEE *puts the photograph back into his wallet.*

ARTHUR Hello.

MELISSA Hello Arthur.

ARTHUR Would you like a drink?

MELISSA No thanks.

ARTHUR Something to eat?

MELISSA I'm fine thank you.

> ARTHUR *takes out his wallet.*

> ARTHUR *holds out a note for* LEE.

ARTHUR *(to* LEE*)* D'you mind getting us a coffee? *(To* MELISSA*)* Sure you don't want something?

MELISSA No thank you.

> LEE *takes the note.*

> *Exit* LEE.

ARTHUR How are you?

MELISSA Y'know. Y'self?

> ARTHUR *nods.*

How's York?

ARTHUR Lovely. Should come.

MELISSA Bit busy at the moment.

ARTHUR Got a job in the Minster. Big cathedral they've got up there.

MELISSA Know what the Minster is.

ARTHUR Bell-ringer.

MELISSA What?

> ARTHUR *nods.*

Y'joking?

> ARTHUR *shakes his head:*

ARTHUR 's great. Took a bit of getting used to.

MELISSA 's it paid?

ARTHUR Not at the moment, but—

MELISSA What ya doin for money?

ARTHUR This and that.

MELISSA Specifically.

ARTHUR Sandwich shop, odd bit of cleaning here and there.

> **MELISSA** *nods.*
>
> Congratulations, by the way. Beautiful name. Lilly. Y'gran's name wasn't it?
>
> *No response.*
>
> Y'brother showed me a photo.
>
> **ARTHUR** *watches* **MELISSA**.
>
> Melissa.
>
> *No response.*
>
> Melissa I'd like to help. I'd like to help you in any way that I can.
>
> *No response.*
>
> D'you understand?
>
> *No response.*
>
> I'd like to help you get back on top of things.

MELISSA Are you seeing someone?

ARTHUR ...

MELISSA You are aren't you?

> **ARTHUR** *nods.*
>
> How long?

ARTHUR Year or so.

MELISSA You living together?

>ARTHUR *shakes his head.*

She married?

No response.

She is isn't she? Home-wrecker.

>MELISSA *watches* ARTHUR.

D'you love her?

>ARTHUR *looks at* MELISSA.

>ARTHUR *nods.*

You do?

>ARTHUR *nods.*

Does she love you?

ARTHUR No idea.

MELISSA Don't believe you.

>ARTHUR *watches* MELISSA.

ARTHUR Yes.

MELISSA She does?

ARTHUR Yes.

>MELISSA *watches* ARTHUR.

MELISSA You look different. Wonder if it's just love?

ARTHUR Y'brother says you've been on something? Taking something. That right?

>MELISSA *nods.*

Is that what.

>ARTHUR *watches* MELISSA.

Melissa I'd really like to help. Kills me seeing ya like this.

MELISSA Know how ya feel.

ARTHUR I mean it.

MELISSA I know you do.

ARTHUR Worst nightmare.

MELISSA What d'you wanna do?

ARTHUR Move back down.

MELISSA What about the bell-ringing?

MELISSA and ARTHUR smile a little.

I don't know Arthur.

ARTHUR What?

MELISSA ...

ARTHUR What don't you know?

MELISSA All sorts of things.

ARTHUR Go on.

MELISSA Well I don't really know you for one.

ARTHUR Neither do I love.

MELISSA Well if that's really true, how can I trust ya?

ARTHUR You can't.

MELISSA Not sure y'really selling y'self.

ARTHUR Just being honest with ya.

MELISSA What d'you propose we do then?

ARTHUR Get you outta this fucking place for starters.

MELISSA Quite like it m'self.

ARTHUR Mean it. Get you home, run you a bath –

MELISSA Bath?

ARTHUR *nods.*

A bath?

ARTHUR *nods.*

ARTHUR Tell me what to say?

MELISSA ...

ARTHUR Not leaving ya. Like this. Can't.

MELISSA Might have to I'm afraid.

ARTHUR Please.

MELISSA What would you like to say?

ARTHUR There's too much.

MELISSA Try.

> **MELISSA** *watches* **ARTHUR**, *she is serious.*

ARTHUR I'm sorry.

Beat.

I'm sorry and I'd like to help.

MELISSA What're you sorry about?

ARTHUR Love.

MELISSA Specifically.

ARTHUR I'm sorry you've not been looked after.

> **MELISSA** *waits.*

I'm sorry I've not looked after you.

MELISSA Why?

ARTHUR ...

MELISSA Why're you sorry?

ARTHUR Because you deserve better.

MELISSA Why?

ARTHUR Because. Because. Because you do.

> **MELISSA** *shakes her head.*
>
> You do though.
>
> *Beat.*
>
> Love I dunno what you want me to say?

MELISSA Just not done your job really, have you?

> **ARTHUR** *shakes his head.*
>
> Have you?

ARTHUR No.

MELISSA Have you?

ARTHUR No.

MELISSA No what?

ARTHUR Love.

MELISSA No what Arthur?

ARTHUR No I have not done my job.

MELISSA Sorry?

ARTHUR Love.

> **MELISSA** *waits.*
>
> You're right. I've not done my job. And I'm sorry. But can we just—

MELISSA Say it again.

ARTHUR Love please.

> **MELISSA** *shakes her head, waits.*
>
> **ARTHUR** *clears his throat.*
>
> I have not done my job.

MELISSA Again.

ARTHUR I have not done my job.

MELISSA Again.

ARTHUR Love what're you doing?

No response.

Please.

MELISSA Again.

ARTHUR I have not done my job.

MELISSA Your what?

ARTHUR My job.

MELISSA Sorry?

ARTHUR My job, I have not done my job.

MELISSA Because?

ARTHUR ...

MELISSA Y'job, why haven't you done it?

ARTHUR Because I'm a cunt.

MELISSA A what?

ARTHUR A cunt. I have not done my job because I'm a *cunt*.

Beat.

MELISSA This woman y'with, you gonna leave her?

ARTHUR No.

MELISSA You're not?

ARTHUR Absolutely not.

MELISSA What about me?

ARTHUR Never.

MELISSA Y'not?

ARTHUR Never.

MELISSA How y'gonna look after the both of us?

ARTHUR What?

MELISSA The both of us, how ya gonna manage to look after the both of us?

ARTHUR Dunno.

MELISSA You don't know?

ARTHUR Love I don't understand

>**ARTHUR** *moves to the holdall, unzips it and takes out the astronaut's helmet last seen in "DECEMBER, 1979".*

I have carted this fucking thing around for thirty plus years. I am sorry. Do you understand? I am sorry and I want to make amends.

MELISSA Was I a mistake?

ARTHUR Love.

MELISSA Did you want me?

>**ARTHUR** *pauses.*

ARTHUR No.

MELISSA Why not?

ARTHUR Love.

MELISSA Why not?

ARTHUR We were a mess.

MELISSA Did you love me?

ARTHUR …

MELISSA Once you had me, did you love me?

ARTHUR Course.

MELISSA Even though you didn't want me?

ARTHUR Of course. Love, Christ, of course. Course we loved you.

MELISSA You did?

ARTHUR Yes.

MELISSA Promise?

ARTHUR Love.

MELISSA Do you promise?

ARTHUR Course we loved you, of course we did.

MELISSA Not we, you. You, did you love me?

> ARTHUR *goes to speak. Doesn't.*
>
> MELISSA *watches* ARTHUR.
>
> ARTHUR *looks at* MELISSA.

ARTHUR I am so sorry.

MELISSA Least you're honest.

ARTHUR I didn't know what it was, I didn't know what to do.

MELISSA It's alright.

ARTHUR You have to understand though—

MELISSA It's alright. The thing that drove me crazy was thinking you loved us.

ARTHUR Love.

MELISSA But you didn't, you didn't. And that's fine—

ARTHUR Love please—

MELISSA No it is, it's fine. Because I don't either.

> MELISSA *takes the astronaut's helmet and gives it to* ARTHUR.

Why don't you hang on to it?

ARTHUR Can I write to you?

MELISSA *nods.*

And Lilly?

MELISSA Yeah.

ARTHUR And if ever there's anything you need, you will—

MELISSA Yeah.

ARTHUR Mean it, anything. Let me give you the e-mail.

ARTHUR rummages through his pockets.

ARTHUR takes out a small business card (the kind printed off at a large supermarket).

MELISSA takes the business card and reads it.

MELISSA "King Arthur one nine four eight".

ARTHUR All other names were gone. Will use it won't ya?

MELISSA *nods.*

Love to Lilly.

MELISSA *nods.*

Exit MELISSA.

ARTHUR clutches the astronaut's helmet.

Enter LEE *with coffee.*

LEE *(meaning astronaut's helmet)* Fuck's that?

ARTHUR 's y'sister's.

LEE holds out the coffee for ARTHUR.

ARTHUR clutches the astronaut's helmet.

LEE sips the coffee.

LEE So what'd she say?

ARTHUR clutches the astronaut's helmet.

MAY, 2008.

MELISSA, *Thirty eight's bedroom. Day. The curtains are drawn.*

MELISSA *sits on the bed, just woken up.*

MELISSA *rubs her eyes.*

MELISSA *takes a glass of water from the bedside table, drinks it.*

MELISSA *puts the glass back.*

MELISSA *opens one of the drawers on the bedside table.*

MELISSA *looks at what's inside the drawer.*

MELISSA *goes to take what's inside the drawer, doesn't.*

MELISSA *shuts the drawer.*

Front door sounds offstage.

RICHARD *(offstage)* Hello.

RICHARD *runs up the stairs.*

MELISSA *stands, runs her hands over her hair, straightening it.*

RICHARD *knocks on the door:*

MELISSA Come in.

Enter RICHARD, *thirty eight.*

MELISSA *and* RICHARD *smile politely at one another.*

Good weekend?

RICHARD *nods.*

RICHARD Mmm.

MELISSA How was Whipsnade?

RICHARD Didn't go in the end.

MELISSA Oh.

RICHARD Laura had to buy a present for her sister's wedding. Left it til the last minute.

MELISSA What did you do?

RICHARD Went to Hamleys.

MELISSA Hamleys?

RICHARD Yeah.

MELISSA The toy shop?

RICHARD Do everything now.

MELISSA What about Lilly?

RICHARD She came with us.

MELISSA Into London?

RICHARD Yeah.

MELISSA Was she alright?

RICHARD Course. She loved it.

MELISSA Did you take her on the underground?

RICHARD Yeah.

MELISSA And she was alright?

RICHARD She was fine. You alright?

MELISSA *nods a little.*

RICHARD *watches* MELISSA.

Promised Lilly I wouldn't say anything, but. She told me about Arthur. Only mention it because I know what it's like and, thought I should say in case there's anything you need, anything I can do.

MELISSA Where's Lilly?

RICHARD Just in the garden. Are you sure you're alright?

MELISSA Not really sure who to invite.

RICHARD Well, Laura and I'll be there. If you'll have us.

MELISSA Course.

RICHARD Lee, Lilly. What about his friends from York?

MELISSA Dunno. Don't really know them.

RICHARD Well look if you wanna put me in touch with some of 'em, happy to give 'em a ring.

MELISSA Thank you. So Laura's sister's getting—

RICHARD Yeah.

MELISSA How old is she?

RICHARD Couple of years younger than Laura. Something I wanted to ask your opinion on actually. D'you mind?

MELISSA *shakes her head a little.*

RICHARD *takes from his pocket a small black box.*

RICHARD *holds out the box in front of* MELISSA *and opens it. Engagement ring.*

MELISSA *covers her mouth with her hand.*

What d'you think?

MELISSA Think it's beautiful.

RICHARD Really?

MELISSA Absolutely.

RICHARD Antique apparently. Sister helped me choose it.

> **RICHARD** *shuts the box and retracts it.*

Sorry is this weird?

MELISSA What?

RICHARD Me showing you my—

MELISSA Of course not.

RICHARD It's not?

MELISSA Course it's not. Really happy for you.

> **MELISSA** *looks ever so slightly tearful.*

RICHARD You like Laura don't you?

> **MELISSA** *nods.*

Yeah?

> **MELISSA** *nods, smiles a little.*

You would say though wouldn't you? If you thought she was a bit of a shit?

MELISSA She's not a shit, Richard.

RICHARD Sure?

MELISSA Think she's wonderful.

RICHARD Lilly seems to like her.

> **MELISSA** *nods.*

> **MELISSA** *grows a little more tearful.*

Sorry. Christ, I'm sorry.

MELISSA It's fine.

RICHARD Just. What you think is so important to me.

MELISSA *nods.*

I mean it. If you thought Laura was a. You know, there's no way I'd—

MELISSA I know.

RICHARD I mean it though.

MELISSA *nods.*

Let me help. With the funeral. Let me help.

MELISSA *nods, tearful.*

You sure you're alright?

MELISSA Started emailing each other. Sending each other photos. Have you ever been to York?

RICHARD *shakes his head a little.*

I wanted go to York Richard. I wanted to see him.

RICHARD *hugs* MELISSA.

They separate.

MELISSA *wipes her eyes.*

Think he'd really changed y'know. Think he really meant it. Everything he said, think he really meant it.

RICHARD Yeah.

MELISSA D'you think I'm a good mother?

RICHARD What?

MELISSA A good mother, d'you think I'm a—

RICHARD Course. Course I think you're a good—

MELISSA D'you really though?

RICHARD Lilly loves you Lis.

MELISSA But d'you think I'm good at it?

RICHARD *nods.*

Y'know I think I understand it now. How he felt, when he left, think I understand it. 'bout feeling safe isn't it? Looked after. Isn't it?

RICHARD *nods a little.*

D'you think she feels safe?

RICHARD ...

MELISSA Lilly, d'you think she feels safe?

RICHARD Should open the curtains, get a bit of light in. Beautiful day.

Beat.

MELISSA So when're y'gonna do it?

RICHARD ...

MELISSA Proposal, when're y'thinking of—

RICHARD Right, God, yeah, dunno. Hadn't really thought about it. God knows what I'm gonna say?

MELISSA Think just tell her you love her.

RICHARD Sort of feel as if I should write something down?

MELISSA Just tell her how you feel, you'll be fine.

RICHARD What d'you think about the knee thing? Mean going down, d'you think it's still the done thing?

MELISSA Think so. Not sure.

RICHARD Not really sure whether Laura's that keen on all that sort of stuff.

MELISSA I liked it.

Silence.

RICHARD Better get going.

MELISSA Yeah.

RICHARD Got a bit of—

MELISSA Yeah.

RICHARD Next weekend though? Still okay for Sunday?

MELISSA Yeah.

RICHARD nods.

RICHARD Thanks again for all the—

MELISSA 's fine.

RICHARD And seriously, I mean it, if you need any help with the, sorting out the, just have to—

MELISSA I will. Thanks.

RICHARD nods a little.

RICHARD moves to go.

RICHARD Open the fucking curtains. Beautiful out there.

Exit RICHARD.

MELISSA watches him go.

MELISSA moves toward the bed.

MELISSA looks at the bedside table.

MELISSA moves the window and pulls back the curtains, warm sunlight streams in.

Enter LILLY, six.

LILLY holds a small box

LILLY is un-noticed by MELISSA, still at the window.

MELISSA turns around:

MELISSA Hello. Have you had a nice weekend?

LILLY *nods.*

LILLY *holds out the box for* MELISSA *to take.*

MELISSA What's this?

MELISSA *opens the box.*

MELISSA Sweetheart. Looks lovely.

LILLY *sits on the floor, still holding the box.*

MELISSA Shouldn't we go and get some plates?

LILLY *shakes her head.*

MELISSA How are we gonna eat it?

LILLY *gestures, "with our hands"*

LILLY *takes* MELISSA*'s hand and gently lowers her to the floor.*

LILLY *opens the box, sticks her hands in.* LILLY *removes them and hands a lump of cake to* MELISSA.

MELISSA *watches* LILLY *as she does the same again for herself.*

LILLY *looks at* MELISSA *before taking her first bite.*

MELISSA Thank you.

LILLY *eats,* MELISSA *watches.*

ABOUT THE AUTHOR

Nick Payne's plays include: *If There Is I Haven't Found It Yet* (Bush Theatre and Roundabout Theatre Company, New York), *Constellations* (Royal Court Theatre, Duke of York's and UK tour, and Manhattan Theatre Club, New York), *The Same Deep Water As Me* (Donmar Warehouse, nominated for 2014 Olivier Award for Best New Comedy), *Incognito* (Nabokov/Live Theatre, Newcastle and Manhattan Theatre Club, New York), *Elegy* (Donmar Warehouse, nominated for 2017 Olivier Award for Best New Play) and *A Life* (Public Theatre, New York and Hudson Theatre, New York). For film, *The Sense of an Ending* (adaptation of Julian Barnes' Man Booker Prize winning novel for BBC Films/Origin Pictures). For television, *Wanderlust* (six-part series for BBC One/Netflix).

**Other plays by NICK PAYNE
published and licensed by Concord Theatricals**

Constellations

Electra

If There Is I Haven't Found It Yet

Incognito

One Day When We Were Young

The Same Deep Water As Me

Wanderlust

**FIND PERFECT PLAYS TO PERFORM AT
www.concordtheatricals.co.uk**

Lightning Source UK Ltd.
Milton Keynes UK
UKHW021626160421
382087UK00007BA/540